SEQUENCES OF EARTH & SPACE

Rivers

Andres Llamas Ruiz

Illustrations by Francisco Arredondo

Sterling Publishing Co., Inc.
New York

Ilustrations by Francisco Arredondo
Text by Andres Llamas Ruiz
Translated by Natalia Tizón

Library of Congress Cataloging-in-Publication Data

Llamas Ruiz, Andrés.
   [Río. English]
   Rivers / Andres Llamas Ruiz.
      p.   cm. — (Sequences of earth & space)
   Includes index.
   Summary: An illustrated description of the creation, types, stages, and effects of rivers.
   ISBN 0-8069-9310-3
   1. Rivers—Juvenile literature. [1. Rivers.] I. Title. II. Series: Llamas Ruiz, Andrés.   Secuencias de la tierra y el espacio. English.
GB1203.8.L5613   1996
523.48´3—dc20
                                  96–9198
                                  CIP
                                  AC

I1 3 5 7 9 10 8 6 4 2

Published by Sterling Publishing Company, Inc.
387 Park Avenue South, New York, N.Y. 10016
Originally published in Spain by Ediciones Estes
©1996 by Ediciones Estes, S.A. ©1996 by Ediciones Lema, S.L.
English version and translation © 1996 by Sterling Publishing Company, Inc.
Distributed in Canada by Sterling Publishing
℅ Canadian Manda Group, One Atlantic Avenue, Suite 105
Toronto, Ontario, Canada M6K 3E7
Distributed in Great Britain and Europe by Cassell PLC
Wellington House, 125 Strand, London WC2R 0BB, England
Distributed in Australia by Capricorn Link (Australia) Pty Ltd.
P.O. Box 6651, Baulkham Hills, Business Centre, NSW 2153, Australia
Printed and Bound in Spain

Sterling ISBN 0-8069-9310-3

Table of Contents

Rain and Snow in the Mountains

Many rivers start their life as winter snow high in the mountains. As the snow begins to melt, it sends streams of water pouring down the mountainsides. At first, all the water filters into the ground. Then, the spring rains add their contributions. Under the impact of the raindrops, pores in the ground gradually fill up, which causes them to close. As the land becomes soaked with water, excess rain runs down along the mountain's surface to form run-off waters.

This water—called mountain stream water—first runs down without being channeled to form minor streams. As the water runs, it causes erosion, tearing away matter from the mountain side and carrying it into the valleys.

Various streams of run-off water join together to form little creeks; as they merge, they form larger rivers. However, as the land dries out, a great part of this water seeps into the ground and feeds into subterranean water supplies.

1. At first, all of the water filters into the ground pores and cracks.
2. If the rain persists, the pores in the ground fill up, gradually closing under the impact of the raindrops.
3. Then the mountain-stream water runs freely without forming major riverbeds.

Rivers form a network that picks up water in the hydrographic basins and takes it to the sea. These hydrographic basins can vary greatly in size, from a few acres (hectares) to half a continent.

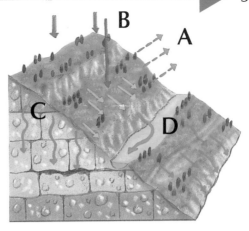

A great deal of rainfall never forms a river. It is lost because of various factors:

A. Evaporation
B. Blockage
C. Filtration
D. Retention

4. If there is no plant life to protect the ground, the water forms a thin layer that carries soil away.

5. In the forests, the water runs hidden under the vegetal cover.

A River Is Born

How is a river born?

Rivers form in channels that collect rainfall or spring water. As water runs down a mountainside, several streams join together and carve out a permanent bed. These narrow creeks are shallow, with fast-running, bubbly water that makes a great deal of noise as it rushes over rocks in the creek bed. If the bed carries water year-round, it is called a river; if it carries water only during certain seasons, it is called a torrent.

During the first part of the river's course, the edges of the rocks over which water flows are covered with lichens. These are the only plants that can withstand the water's force. In fact, the streams run so fast that only those insects that can hold onto the lichen-covered rocks can survive.

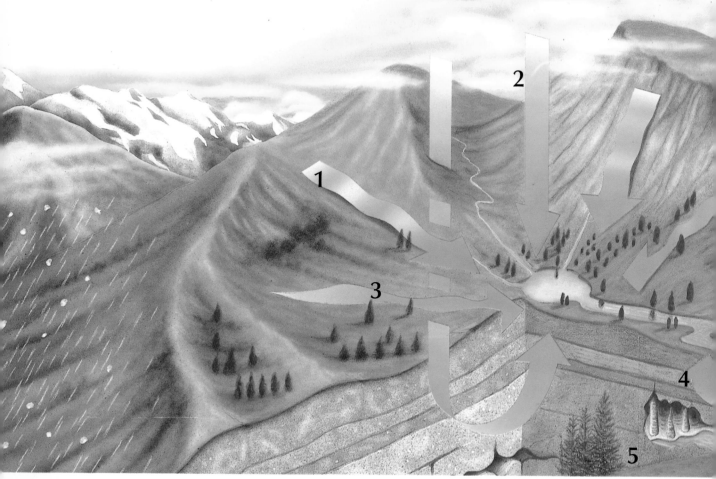

River water that comes from rain, filtration, or snow and glacier melts can leave the basin several different ways.

1. Rainwater runs down the mountainsides of the hydrographic basin.

2. Water may also fall directly into the river.

When snow starts to melt in the spring, water flows down the mountainsides.

One spectacular way that rivers develop is through eruptions from the earth's interior.

3. When there are dense rocks, practically all water joins surface drainage routes and runs down the mountain inside.

4. Water can also run toward the river just under the surface.

5. Water can filter underground and travel until it comes back out to the surface.

The First Stage: High Mountain Creeks

The first stage of a river runs as a creek, streaming down a steep mountainside, in a bed formed of large stones. The water is cold, poor in nutrients, and carries few minerals. There is very little lichen at this stage, since the force of the stream carries pebbles that erode the bottom of the bed. In fact, life in this water is almost nonexistent; it may include bacteria, encrusted algae, and insect larvae.

A few deep pools are distributed along this portion of the river. Trout—one of the few fish strong enough to swim against the powerful stream—can be found here. Every so often during a flood, neighboring animal and plant communities will be dragged into the stream. In time, new inhabitants will start their hard life, fighting against the force of the stream.

1. The river runs steep and strong, with great eroding power.

2. The riverbed is formed by rocks and pebbles, which do not allow plants to grow.

3. The first stage of the river displays great eroding power by digging up the bed.

If the water flows on a hard, rocky surface, it can form huge gorges.

After its first few miles, the river's banks fill with plant life. The leaves and branches that fall into the river are a source of nutrients, matter, and energy.

4. Stones and dead branches sitting in the water and exposed to the light are covered by a jelly-like layer of thousands of microscopic algae called diatomaceous algae.

5. Plants may prevent sunlight from reaching the river.

Waterfalls and Cascades

Have you ever seen a waterfall?

Waterfalls and cascades are very common along the first part of a river's course. The water falls with a deafening crash from high up, managing its way among abrupt changes in gradient.

How were these uneven lands formed? There are many possibilities. Variations in inclination may be due to a fault (a fracture in the earth's crust that can be millions of years old).

Cascades are caused by the different resistance among various kinds of rocks. They are formed when the water goes from one hard rock that resists the water's erosion to a softer rock that is easily eroded.

Waterfalls are often formed when a river flows through areas of different surface hardness. If the water first runs through hard and then soft material, the latter erodes very quickly and an abrupt change in inclination is created.

1. Water falls heavily from a very high point, making a noise that can be heard from far away.

Rivers can carry materials in several different ways:

A. *Vegetal remains, for example, float down-river.*
B. *Soluble substances are dissolved in water.*
C. *Small particles are suspended in the river.*
D. *Fragments are moved easily.*
E. *Heavy materials are dragged or rolled along the river bottom.*

The "Horse Tail" waterfall, over 144 feet (44 meters) tall, "grows" in a very special way. Falling water (a) gradually erodes the materials at the base to form a kind of "cap" that will, in time, end up collapsing (b).

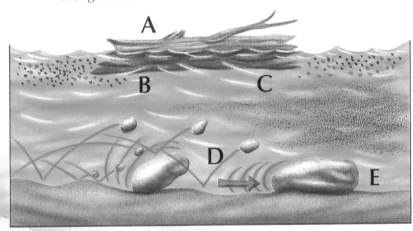

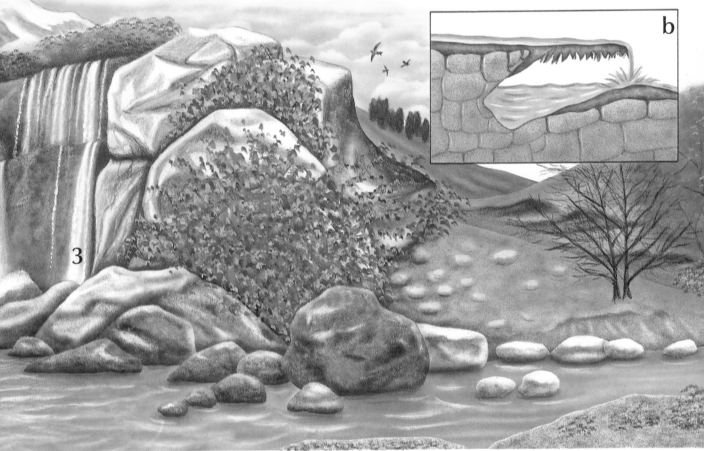

2. As it falls through gorges, water wears away the materials underneath it. In this way, the water remains falling vertically even as time goes by.

3. Year after year, the river erodes away the edges of the waterfall, which "wears out" and recedes.

The Middle Stage

Rivers increase as creeks join and mix to form deeper beds. Gradually, the bed widens, its inclination decreases, and the water runs more slowly as the river flows out of the mountains. Consequently, the river has less capacity to carry materials. In areas where the water is calmest, materials will be deposited along the riverbed; the resulting piles of gravel help encourage the growth of water plants.

During its middle stage, the river bottom has changed greatly. Its stones are much smaller and made round from wear. They are frequently covered by algae and lichen. As you can see, during the middle stage, conditions are favorable for plant life along the riverbanks and in the water.

The river now has many insects (such as dragonflies and caddis flies) and fish (such as trout, salmon, eel, etc).

As the river flows toward the sea, it widens and slows down.

1. A moderately fast-running river deposits stones but continues to carry along sand and mud.

2. When the speed of the river decreases, piles of gravel form along the banks; a slow-moving river cannot keep such material moving. It is

Beavers can change the river-scape drastically by building dams where water levels are constant so that much of the debris carried by the river will be deposited.

Rivers have an incredible eroding force. For thousands of years, their erosion continues to carve out new forms, creating such spectacular sights as the Grand Canyon.

here that plants, such as buttercups, will grow.

3. When the river's water rises, the closest plains are flooded. That is why they are called floodplains.

4. The stones are now much smaller and their edges have been rounded off.

The Riverbanks

The riverbanks change gradually as the river follows its course to the sea. You have already seen that, during the first stage, the river runs very fast over the rocks. As the river slows down, the riverbed widens and its banks soften. The banks of lakes and ponds also have soft ground where many types of plants grow.

If the river is very wide, it slows down so completely that many plants take root near the banks. The plants have very strong roots to resist flooding during the rainy seasons.

Willows, whose flexible trunks make them resistant to rising water, grow closest to the river. These trees are very important, since their roots hold the ground and help prevent erosion.

As the nature of the banks begins to change, the plants and animals that inhabit them also change. For example, reeds develop only in areas where there is slow-running water.

Along the riverbanks, plants are distributed in rows, depending on their needs. Periodic flooding also makes those plants that live next to the river adapt to changing conditions.

1. Along the riverbanks, the constant presence of water makes it possible for deciduous trees to grow, even

Scientists have discovered that the conditions at a certain point of the river can change from one bank to the other. You can see here how, as the strength of the river changes, plant life along the riverbed also changes.

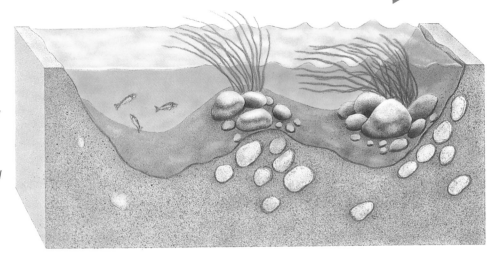

when they are very far from their normal climates.

2. The composition of the ground along the banks varies, since it is formed by different kinds of material deposited by the river.

3. Many animals dig tunnels along the riverbanks and make their burrows there.

A Lake Is Formed

The river cannot always reach the sea. You have already seen that water can be lost in a crevice, although it can also be retained to form a lake. Normally, a "lake" is a body of water that has a certain minimal depth. If it is not very deep, it is called a lagoon or pond.

Most lakes are formed by geological processes. For example, the last glaciation is responsible for creating a great number of lakes that now occupy positions that were once large masses of ice. Volcanic activity also creates lakes. It is even thought that some lakes were formed when meteorites crashed into the earth's surface, leaving behind large craters that eventually filled with water.

Did you know that lakes grow old and die? As time goes by, they fill up with the waste and sediments carried by the water. After many years, as plant life gradually gains ground, a thick forest forms where there was once a lake.

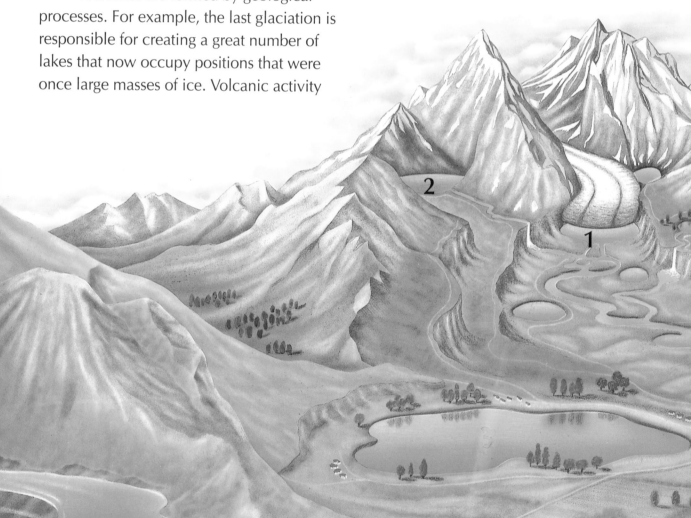

Lakes are born, grow old, and die. The destiny of every lake depends on many factors, such as its origin, its size and shape, the weather in the area where it is located, etc. If the lake forms on hard, rocky ground with few nutrients, it will "grow old" much more slowly.

1. Some lakes originated when water accumulated in holes created by glacial ice.

Many high mountain lakes spend the winter covered with a thick layer of ice.

The fate of all lakes is to disappear completely when they are covered by sediment and vegetation. In old lakes, the banks are covered by abundant amounts of plant life.

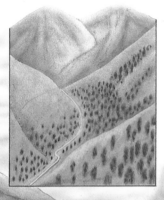

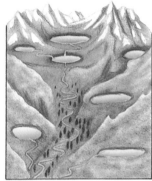

You can see here how some mountain lakes are formed from old glaciers. The ponds are staggered in valleys that, in earlier ages, were covered with ice.

2. In front of and next to a glacier, lakes can form if the water produced from melting ice is retained.

3. A lake can also be created by volcanic action.

4. Some lakes are supported by a subterranean water supply.

Temporary Ponds

Sometimes, water becomes trapped to form ponds. These are small water systems that usually collect on impermeable ground. However, their small size makes them vulnerable to weather changes and seasonal variations.

Even if they are very small, ponds contain a surprising variety of life. The best season to observe a pond is in the spring, when many plants bloom and animals wake from their winter sleep.

Like lakes, ponds do not remain the same from year to year. Mud and dead plants accumulate at the bottom. Then, as the depth of the pond decreases, the reeds on the banks grow closer to the pond. If this process continues, the pond will become first a marsh, then a field, and then a forest.

1

2

A "temporary" pond experiences many changes throughout the year. During the dry seasons, it may dry up completely. The plants and animals that live in these ponds have to develop special ways to survive when the water disappears.

1. Some species lay eggs that are capable of surviving drought.

Some temporary ponds occupy vast areas, even though they are much shallower than a lake.

This is the distribution of some of the inhabitants of a mountain pond. As you can see, there is a variety of animals as well as plant organisms.

3

2. Water plants and single-cell algae leave their seeds and spores buried in the mud.

3. When the pond fills with water again, everything comes back to life.

The Final Stage of the River

In this stage, the width and volume of the river, together with a small incline and increase in depth, create new living conditions for organisms. During its journey, the river has been receiving water from many tributaries that are sometimes as big as the river itself. In its final stages, the river widens and its bottom is covered by silt and mud. Algae can no longer live in the water. This is because the water now carries many parti-

cles and sediments, which makes it difficult for sunlight to penetrate its surface. However, areas where the stream is slower provide home for plankton, which is formed by microscopic algae that dye the water a darkgreen color.

The water runs slowly, especially along the banks where mud accumulates and reeds grow abundantly. All of these plants have strong roots that hold onto the bottom, resisting rises in water after a rain. The reeds that grow next to the slow-water areas of a river's lower stage are an excellent refuge for water birds.

1

Rivers never run straight. Their sharp turns are called meanders. In its final stage, the river carries finer sediments and its volume is more regular, which creates wide meanders.

1. The two banks of a river with meanders are very different. One bank curves out, leading gently down to a

In part of its course, the river seems totally disoriented. There are meanders everywhere and the water doesn't seem to follow any clear direction.

A

B

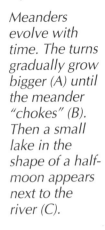

C

Meanders evolve with time. The turns gradually grow bigger (A) until the meander "chokes" (B). Then a small lake in the shape of a half-moon appears next to the river (C).

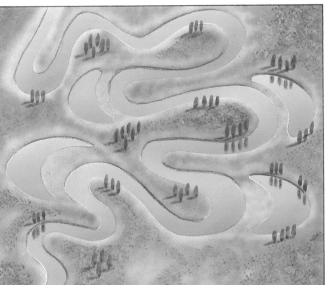

2

riverbed covered by sand and pebbles that were deposited by the weakened river.

2. The other bank curves in and is much more vertical, because it is eroded by the force of the river.

Swamp Areas

Often, in this part of the river there are places in which the water seems to have lost its way. It is hard to know where the river ends and the land begins. These areas can have different names: marshes, mudflats, or swamps. Each of them has its own character-istics. For example, some of them look like lakes, while others look like prairies covered with reeds.

Normally, these places lie on both sides of a wide but not very deep river, although the swamp areas can contain either fresh. or saltwater. Freshwater swamp areas are often located close to lakes or lagoons. They may also develop close to big rivers that flood every year. Saltwater swamp areas are in coastal regions, close to the estuary and mouth of a river because the saltwater comes from the sea.

1

Swamp areas, such as marshes, can change in water level depending on the seasons, but plants and animals have adapted so well that life there is very abundant. Grass and reeds provide refuge for a large number of animals, such as alligators, snakes, and especial-ly birds.

1. The stream is so slow that the water seems to have completely stopped.

Marshes are lands that lie just above sea level. They are crossed by a series of river branches that divide to reunite later, reaching the sea as a single river.

Marshes are created from an old estuary (A) where the river sediments accumulate. First, there are small islands (B) in the estuary. Then the tide brings sand, which, together with mud from the river, forms a large swamp with streams of freshwater crossing through it (C).

A

B

C

3

2

2. There are leaves from many floating plants that rock on the surface of the water.

3. The submerged areas alternate with non-submerged areas without any apparent order.

The River Reaches the Sea

When the river reaches the sea, its two banks gradually separate. The sea is so close that the low and high tides are very noticeable because saltwater enters the river during high tide and mixes with freshwater.

When it reaches the sea, the river suddenly stops its currents as it crashes against the sea. Then, a delta or an estuary may be formed, depending on the tides, current, waves, amount of sediments, etc.

If the materials are not carried away by the ocean's current, they settle and deposit there. They first form a sandbar that will separate into several arms to a make a triangular, or fan-shaped, delta. The river's mouth can also form an estuary that is free of sediment, thanks to the currents caused by the ocean's tides. These estuaries form a wide, deep gulf where the mixing of fresh- and saltwater takes place. Many of them are surrounded by large marsh areas.

The accumulation of sediments at the bottom can create a very special environment, such as coastal lagoons and deltas. In deltas, the land matter that has been carried by the river gradually gains ground. The large number of birds that live in these places is especially noticeable.

1. Both banks separate and become the banks of the sea.

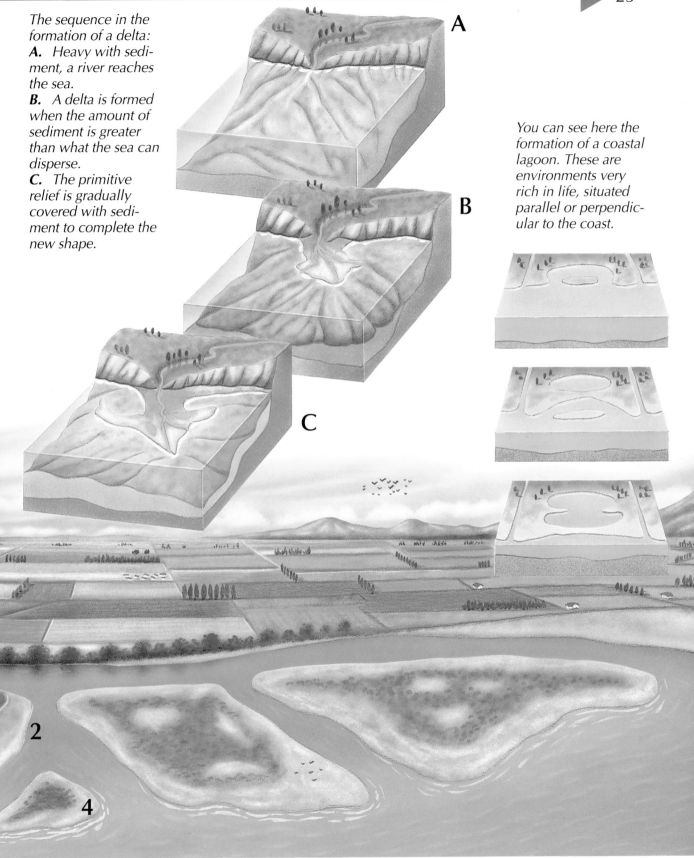

The sequence in the formation of a delta:
A. Heavy with sediment, a river reaches the sea.
B. A delta is formed when the amount of sediment is greater than what the sea can disperse.
C. The primitive relief is gradually covered with sediment to complete the new shape.

A

B

C

You can see here the formation of a coastal lagoon. These are environments very rich in life, situated parallel or perpendicular to the coast.

2

4

2. The river stops and deposits even the smallest particles at the bottom.

3. Twice a day these land forms are covered by saltwater from the sea.

4. During low tides, mud banks become exposed.

The Cycle Begins Again

The river finishes its journey by having its water incorporated into the sea. This, however, is not the end: In fact, this same water will eventually return to the head of the river to start the cycle again as the sun's heat evaporates water from the lakes, rivers, and oceans.

Gas is formed, rising into the atmosphere and creating clouds.

When the water vapor cools down, tiny drops group together to form bigger drops, which finally fall to the earth's surface in the form of rain or snow. This process is known as the "water cycle." The water that the atmosphere drops onto the continents each year "restocks" the rivers.

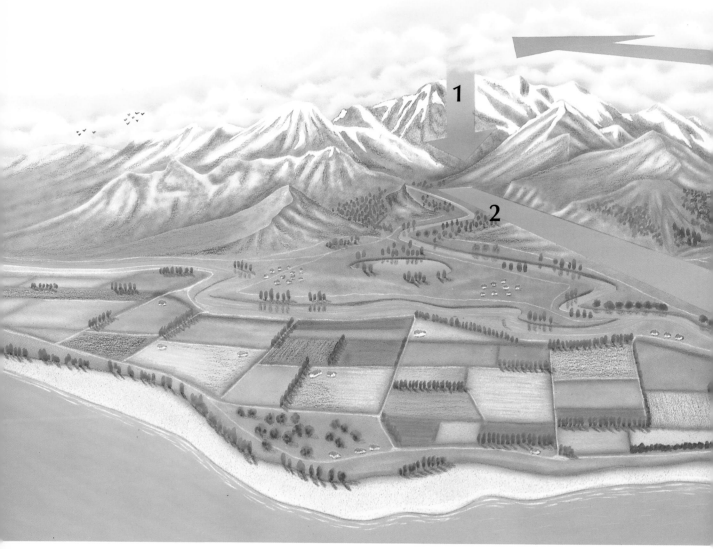

You can see in this illustration the endless water cycle.

1. The water cycle starts when moisture falls on the mountains as snow.

2. When the snow melts, part of the water filters into the ground.

Current river mouths were created about 5,000 million years ago when the sea invaded all lowlands after the glaciers melted. You can see here how an estuary was formed after the sea invaded an old river valley.

3. As we go farther away from the river's headwaters, the water is warmer, the basin is bigger, and the flow decreases.

4. Rivers transport 10,000 million tons of sediment to the sea annually.

5. Water evaporates into the atmosphere, starting the cycle again.

Ice Rivers

Did you know that the biggest rivers on earth are frozen? They are immense rivers of ice called glaciers, which move at less than the speed of a snail. Some of them are gigantic: many miles long, hundreds of feet wide, and covering millions of acres of surface. In fact, glacier ice contains almost 90% of the world's freshwater!

In Greenland, a layer of ice is more than 6,000 feet (2,000 meters) thick. In Antarctica, ice caps can be up to 14,000 feet (4,300 meters) thick!

The speed of a glacier is not uniform. It depends on the physical characteristics of the individual glacier as well as on the seasons. For example, the speed can vary between 82 feet (25 meters) per year for some Swiss glaciers and about 121 feet (37 meters) per day for Alaskan glaciers!

Some glaciers are immense areas of frozen water.

1. The sides of the peaks covered with snow are called "glacial valleys."

2. Heat from the sun melts the surface snow and the water filters downward.

3. The "glacial tongue" decreases in thickness as it goes down.

The glacier reaches the sea to form ice walls that can reach more than 130 feet (40 meters) above sea level. When huge pieces of ice fall off the glacier, icebergs are formed. Icebergs float on the water, although 90% of their mass is under the surface.

You can see here how a lake was formed from a glacier. The ice covered the landscape (A), and the accumulation of earth and stones formed a barrier that now retains the lake water (B), although a small amount escapes through a narrow, shallow bed.

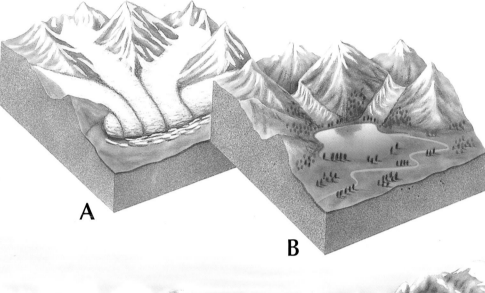

A

B

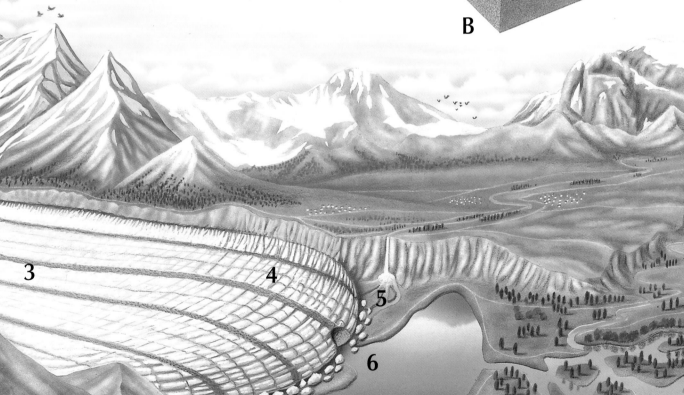

3

4

5

6

4. The surface is lined with very deep crevices.

5. Banks are covered with pebbles and small rocks.

6. A torrent of cold, fast-running water emerges from the front (called a glacial front).

Underground Rivers

Did you know that some rivers run underground, with secondary rivers, lakes and even cascades?

When the water that filters into the ground reaches a layer of impermeable material, it accumulates and forms a layer of water. Over the centuries, these underground streams join to form underground rivers that widen their beds.

The journey of the underground water depends very much on the material that it travels on. For example, in regions of granite, water from rain and melted snow filters through fissures in the rock until it finds an unbreakable barrier. Then, the water circulates along that surface until it comes back out through the rock fissures. This type of water source is common, although it only flows abundantly during the months following rain and snow; it can dry up during the dry season.

Underground rivers are especially important in calcareous regions since the water dissolves the rock to form rivers that circulate through a maze of tunnels and caves.

In calcareous mountains, a river can totally disappear when it reaches a large fissure. The river then becomes an underground current.

1. The water crosses the lands formed by permeable materials and stops when it reaches impermeable layers.

2. Over thousands of years, underground streams join to form rivers that widen their beds.

Inside calcareous mountains, water that filters down from the surface can create large crevices and caves.

Some lagoons are formed by underground water emerging to the surface.

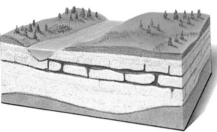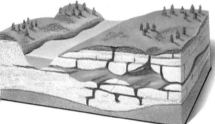

In the calcareous mountains, the water finds a way to cross the crevices in the stones. Then, the rock dissolves and forms tunnels and passages for the water to circulate. In time, the water dissolves more of the mountain.

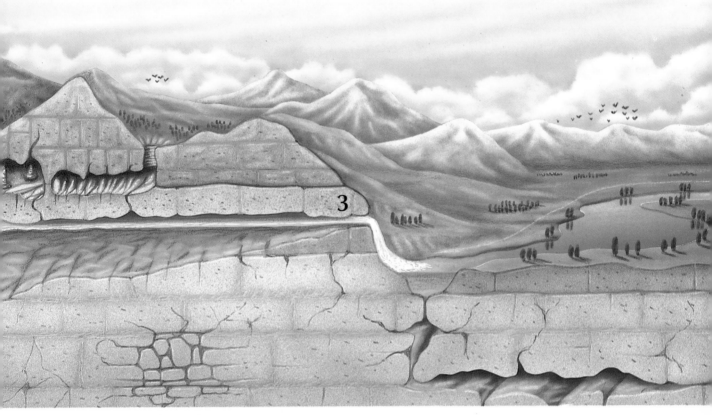

3. When phreatic (groundwater) layers reach the surface of the ground, they create springs.

Glossary

Banks: The sides of a river.

Bed: Where the river flows through.

Calcareous: Made up of or containing calcium carbonate.

Cubic meter: A unit of volume that is equal to a cube whose side measures 1 meter. It is equivalent to 1,000 liters.

Delta: A huge accumulation of sediment into the shape of a triangular island. It is formed at the estuary of some rivers.

Diatomaceous algae: Single-cell algae that live in fresh- or saltwater.

Erosion: The destruction and modeling of the earth's surface that is caused by external geological agents, such as wind, ice, seawater, etc.

Estuary: The part of a river next to the sea that is reached by the tides.

Gravel: Small, crushed stones that can be found parts in different part of riverbeds.

Hectare: Square surface measure that is equal to 100 meters per side.

Hydrographic basins: The area where all the water flows into one river.

Layer of water: It is formed by the accumulation of water traveling underground.

Pebbles: Little stones that lie mainly along the banks of rivers and creeks.

River mouth: A point where the water from the river stream reaches the sea (or another river).

Riverbed: A place through which the river water runs.

Secondary river: A river that comes together with another river, adding more water to it.

Sediment: Matter that, after floating in water, is deposited at the bottom of a river.

Silt: Soft mud that is deposited at the bottom of the rivers, lakes, etc.

Tributary: A stream feeding a larger stream or a lake.

Index

8 - 5/01
17 6/06